First World War
and Army of Occupation
War Diary
France, Belgium and Germany

15 DIVISION
Headquarters, Branches and Services
General Staff
3 July 1915 - 30 July 1915

WO95/1911/2

The Naval & Military Press Ltd
www.nmarchive.com
Published in association with The National Archives

Published by

The Naval & Military Press Ltd

Unit 10 Ridgewood Industrial Park,

Uckfield, East Sussex,

TN22 5QE England

Tel: +44 (0) 1825 749494

www.naval-military-press.com

www.nmarchive.com

This diary has been reprinted in facsimile from the original. Any imperfections are inevitably reproduced and the quality may fall short of modern type and cartographic standards.

© Crown Copyright
Images reproduced by permission of The National Archives, London, England, 2015.

Contents

Document type	Place/Title	Date From	Date To
Heading	WO95/1911/2 15 Div HQ Gen Staff of Depts Jul-Sep 1915 Gen Staff Jul 1915		
Heading	15th Div. G.S. July, 1915		
Miscellaneous	15th Division Headquarters 15th Division (I.S) Vol I. 3-31.7.15		
War Diary	Marlborough	03/07/1915	08/07/1915
War Diary	Folkestone	08/07/1915	08/07/1915
War Diary	Boulougne	09/07/1915	09/07/1915
War Diary	Tilques	09/07/1915	15/07/1915
War Diary	Renescure	15/07/1915	16/07/1915
War Diary	Bourecq	16/07/1915	17/07/1915
War Diary	Gosnay	17/07/1915	30/07/1915
Miscellaneous	15th Division Introduction into Trench Line.		
Miscellaneous	Please see letter no G/317/4 of 23/7/15 forwarded by 47th Divn	23/07/1915	23/07/1915
Miscellaneous	A Form Messages And Signals.	28/07/1915	28/07/1915
Miscellaneous	My only remarks refer to para 3 (d)	26/07/1915	26/07/1915
Miscellaneous	15th Division 64/G Proposed disposition of 15th Div. Art.	25/07/1915	25/07/1915
Miscellaneous	B.G.R.A. DA & QMG		
Miscellaneous	A Form. Messages And Signals.	29/07/1915	29/07/1915
Miscellaneous	Headquarters, 1st Army. 1st Corps XX1st French Corps.	27/07/1915	27/07/1915
Miscellaneous	1st Division. 47th Division. 15th Division.	27/07/1915	27/07/1915
Miscellaneous	Headquarters, 47th Division.	27/07/1915	27/07/1915
Miscellaneous	IVth Corps No. 15th Division	27/07/1915	27/07/1915
Miscellaneous	1st Division. 15th Division. 47th Division.	19/07/1915	19/07/1915
Miscellaneous	Draft. 3 Division.		
Miscellaneous	Artillery-15th Division Showing dates of introduction to 1st Division line for instruction.		
Miscellaneous	4th Corps H.R.S. 303. 15th Division.	24/07/1915	24/07/1915
Miscellaneous	4th Corps H.R.S. 303. 47th Division.	24/07/1915	24/07/1915
Miscellaneous	To Headquarters 47th. (London) Division	22/07/1915	22/07/1915
Miscellaneous	1st Division. 15th Division. 47th Division.	20/07/1915	20/07/1915
Miscellaneous	4th Corps. No. 832 (c). 1st Division. 15th Division. 47th Division.	28/07/1915	28/07/1915
Miscellaneous	1st Divn. No. 394 (G) 4th Corps.	21/07/1915	21/07/1915
Miscellaneous	15th Division 19/G Forwarded for information-your 832/G dated 19/7/15	19/07/1915	19/07/1915
Miscellaneous	15th Division 19/G. 44th/45th/46th Inf. Bdes.	22/07/1915	22/07/1915
Miscellaneous	Table "A" 15th Division 19/G of 20/7/1915	20/07/1915	20/07/1915
Miscellaneous	Table "B" 15th Division 19/G of 20/7/15.	20/07/1915	20/07/1915
Miscellaneous	Table "C" Bus, etc, arrangements.		
Miscellaneous	15th Division 19/G. 44th/45th/46th. Inf. Bdes.	22/07/1915	22/07/1915
Miscellaneous	Table "A" 15th Division 19/G of 20/7/1915	20/07/1915	20/07/1915
Miscellaneous	Table "B" 15th Division 19/G of 20/7/15.	20/07/1915	20/07/1915
Miscellaneous	Table "C" Bus, etc, arrangements.		
Miscellaneous	1st Army Headquarters.	17/07/1915	17/07/1915
Miscellaneous	Record of The 15th. (Scottish) Division.		

WO95/1911-2

15 Div HQ Gen Staff & Depts
Jul–Sep 1915

Gen Staff
Jul 1915

15TH DIV.
G.S.
July, 1915

Dec 1915

101/6149

15th Division

Headquarters 15th Division (95)

Vol. I.

3 — 31.7.15.

Army Form C. 2118

WAR DIARY
or
INTELLIGENCE SUMMARY
(Erase heading not required.)

Instructions regarding War Diaries and Intelligence Summaries are contained in F. S. Regs., Part II. and the Staff Manual respectively. Title Pages will be prepared in manuscript.

P. 1.

Place	Date	Hour	Summary of Events and Information	Remarks and references to Appendices
MARLBOROUGH	3.7.15		15th Division ordered to FRANCE.	
	7.7.15		Entrainment commenced.	
	8.7.15	5.50pm	H.Q. entrained	
FOLKESTONE	"	11.30pm	H.Q. embarked	
BOULOGNE	9.7.15	2.30am	H.Q. disembarked - rested	
TILQUES	"	12.30pm	H.Q. Established - detrainment of Division begins at AUDRUICQ, WATTEN & ST OMER.	
	13.7.15		Division concentrated in area TILQUES - NORTBECOURT - BONNINGUES - LOUCHES - ZUTMERQUE - RUMINGHEM - SERQUES.	
	14.7.15	11.40pm	IV - Corps O/p order No 34 received fixing move up to VI - Corps area.	
	"	1.40pm	G.H.Q. O/p order No OA 528 of 14.7.15 received directing march of Division to Area ARQUES - HAZEBROUCK where it will come under orders of 1st Army	
	"	5.50pm	15th Div. O/p order Issued for above move to ARQUES - HAZEBROUCK area.	
	"	6.30pm	1st Army O/p order No. G.S. 111/6(A) of 14.7.15 received giving over for movement (6th inst.) into AIRE area where Div. will come under orders of IV - Corps.	
	15.7.15	7am	Division marches to ARQUES - HAZEBROUCK area.	
RENESCURE	"	11am	H.Q. Established	
		2.30pm	15th Div O/p Order No 2 issued for move to AIRE area.	

Army Form C. 2118

p. 2.

WAR DIARY
INTELLIGENCE SUMMARY
(Erase heading not required.)

Place	Date	Hour	Summary of Events and Information	Remarks and references to Appendices
PENESCURE	6.7.15	7 a.m.	Division marched to AIRE area.	
		11 a.m.	Amended march table IV- Corps OO over No. 30 of 1/3.7.15, received.	
BOURECQ	"	12 noon	H.Q. established.	
		7.30 p.m.	15th Div OO over No 3 cancels move into IV Corps area. — Heavy rain all night.	
	7.7.15	9 a.m.	Division marches to IV Corps area.	
GOSNAY	"	10.30 a.m.	H.Q. established.	
	"	7 p.m.	All moves of units (except 74th CoRE, 91st CoRE, 44th Inf Bde & 9th Jordans Horse (by night)) reported completed. — Rain nearly all day.	
	8.7.15	11.5 a.m.	All moves reported complete and IV Corps informed of distribution.	
	"	12.55 p.m.	Our battalion 44th Inf Bde to be moved to 1st S.R.E & 1.S for work under CRE, 2nd Ind Cav Div.	
	"	4.10 p.m.	7th Camerons ordered to leave HOUCHIN at 9 p.m.	
	9.7.15	1.15 p.m.	Orders received for introduction of Division to the Trenches.	
	"	2.10 p.m.	Orders received for our battalion to proceed to MAROC — 13.7.15. Sect detailed by 45th I.B. leaving HESDIGNEUL 8.30 p.m.	
	20.7.15	12.30 p.m.	Order for introduction of brigades etc to trenches issued - attachment to arms worked out 29.7.15 — 1.8.15.	

WAR DIARY

INTELLIGENCE SUMMARY

Army Form C. 2118

Place	Date	Hour	Summary of Events and Information	Remarks and references to Appendices
GOSNAY	24/7/15	12.55pm	Drain wains fraternal of RE to 47th Div in trenches.	
	24/7/25		10th Gordon Highrs relieve 7th Cameron Highrs at LISS BRIDGE.	
	25/7/15	9.15am	IVth Corps derelict Thereafter 6am on 27th, 9th Gordon Highrs (Reserve) come under orders of Major CRAFTER, R.E. for work on GRENAY line. Prepared disposition of Division forwards to IVth Corps.	
			11th A. & S. Highrs detailed between ANNEQUIN on 27th inst for work in 1st Bn Area.	
	25/26		6th Cameron Highrs relieves 13th R. Scots at MARCO.	
	27/7/15	10.25am	IVth Corps sanctions of working parties from 9th Gordon Highrs (Reserve) for digging additional R.A Emplacements	
			Orders received Brevies 47th Division in Section W & X by 6 am 4.8.15.	
		12.40pm	Nos 3 and 8 Trench Mortar batteries R.G.A. will be transferred to Div when relief Takes place.	
	29/7/15	12.15pm	3rd Heavy Bde R.G.A., No 7 Anti-Aircraft Section, No 4 - 15" Howitzer, No 3 and 4 - 9.2 Howrs, 15" Siege battery and 2-8" Howrs 19th Siege battery will be attached Div. from Aug 4th.	
	30/7/15	11.30am	Div Op order No 4 for relief by 15th Div of 47th Div in Sectors W, X issued.	
		10.50pm	25th Co. R.E. will be attached to Div from Aug 4th.	

31.7.15.

Mxxxx Lieut Col.
G.S.
for G.O.C. 15th Division

HRS 303

SECRET

Army Form A 2007.

CENTRAL REGISTRY.

303

Central Registry No. and Date.　　　　　　　Attached Files.

SUBJECT, AND OFFICE OF ORIGIN.

15th Division

Introduction into Trench Line.

Referred to	Date	Referred to	Date	Referred to	Date
BGRA to see before despatch AgD	20.7.15				
Seen A.W.					
BGRA AgD	23.7.15			P.A.	Date
G	23/7/15				

Schedule of Correspondence.

Inter-office Minutes.

BGRA

Please see letter no G/317/4 of 23/7/15 forwarded by 47th Div'n.

Do these proposals appear sound to you?

Ask the labour required for the preparation of artillery positions & handing over of cable, Div'ns have already been instructed to arrange matters between them. I propose to forward this mt to 47th Div'n.

AG Dallas
1858

23.7.15

B.G.G.S.

I have discussed this with Gen. Wray, & I think his proposals are quite sound.

AWH

BGGS

The sections should go across from the I Div to their positions in the 47 Div as originally arranged — Wire to be left down and similar amount to be handed over by 15 to 47 Div.

BG

24/7

"A" Form. Army Form C. 2121.
MESSAGES AND SIGNALS.

| TO | 47th Division |
| | 15th Division |

| Sender's Number | Day of Month | In reply to Number | |
| G 383 | 28-7-15 | | AAA |

Number 3 Trench mortar battery and number 8 Trench mortar battery will be transferred from the 47th Division to the 15th Division when relief of line takes place

From 4th Corps
Place
Time 12.40 pm

My only remarks refer to para 3(d) & (e).—

(d) No objection so far as the lines selected are in the Divisional area.

(e) Bois des Dames is not in the area allotted and therefore cannot be used.

J Doyle
A.

26.7.15

Copies to 47th & MGRA. for information –
mad told as

15th Division 64/G.

4th Corps.

Proposed disposition of 15th Div. Art.

1. General Lambart has made a full reconnaissance of the front now occupied by 47th Div., and reports that he can eventually provide emplacements for 12 batteries within that front to succeed the 9 batteries of the 47th Div. now in action. This will still necessitate finding space behind the line for the horses and wagon lines of 3 more batteries than have now to be provided for by the 47th Div., as well as for 4 batteries held in reserve.

2. General Lambart reports that the bivouacs of the Bde: Ammn:Cols: of the 47th Div: in the woods by DROUVIN are overcrowded and the ground very foul; also that water is insufficient for a large number of horses.

3. I propose in the first instance to distribute my Divl. Art: as follows:-

   (a) 12 batteries in action, with Ammn: at hand and sufficient horses to move the guns a short distance.

   (b) Four batteries with gun and wagon teams in reserve behind NOEUX-les-MINES.

   (c) A proportion of Bde: Ammn Cols: about DROUVIN and HOUCHIN.

   (d) Remainder of Bde: Ammn: Cols: and horses and first line wagons not wanted up with batteries, in the valley of the LAWE between M^{in} ROUGE and GOSNAY.

   (e) Div: Ammn: Col: in BOIS-des-DAMES.

4. I beg to request that the billetting area of this Div: as it will be when I take over from the 47th may be exactly defined as soon as possible, as sections of 8 of my batteries will be in action in that area on the 27th instant. I have also to consider the disposal of the transport of the rest of my Div:.

5. As I shall have 8 full batteries of my Div: in action on the night of the 29th/30th inst, may I be informed as to whether my B.G.R.A. is to assume command of the Art: of the sector on that date.

H.Q. 15th Division.

25th July 1915.

Major-General,
Commanding 15th Division.

B.GR.A.
DA & Gen. S.
For remarks if any
A.D.
26.7.15

"A" Form.
MESSAGES AND SIGNALS.
Army Form C. 2121.

TO: 47th Division

Sender's Number	Day of Month	In reply to Number	
G 406	29/7/15		AAA

Reference 4th Corps telegram G 383 yesterdays date 47th Division will also hand over to 15th Division six 95 millimetre mortars AAA addressed 47th and 15th Divisions

From: Fourth Corps
Place:
Time: 10.40 am

Lt A.J. Dallas

"A" Form.   Army Form C. 2121.
MESSAGES AND SIGNALS.   No. of Message_____

| Prefix____Code____m. | Words | Charge | This message is on a/c of | Recd. at____m. |
| Office of Origin and Service Instructions. | Sent At____m. To____ By____ | | _____Service. (Signature of "Franking Officer.") | Date____ From____ By____ |

TO: 4th Division
    15th Division

Sender's Number.	Day of Month	In reply to Number	
G404	29-7-15		AAA

The 3rd Heavy Brigade R.G.A. will be transferred from the 4th Division to the 15th Division when the latter assumes responsibility for the Defence of the line and Number 14 Anti-aircraft Section will be administered by the 15th Division with effect from the 4th instant but will remain for tactical purposes under direct orders of the 4th Corps aaa Number 4 - 15" Howitzer and Numbers 3 and 4 13" Siege Battery and 2 eight inch Hows of 19th Siege Battery will be attached to 15th Division for administration from the 4th inst aaa Ammn returns of 15 inch 9 point 2 and eight inch Hows will continue to be rendered through 1st Corps.

From: 4th Corps
Place: ____
Time: 10.45am

                                      A.G. Dallas B.G.G.S.

"A" Form.
MESSAGES AND SIGNALS.
Army Form C. 2121.

TO: 47th Division

Sender's Number: G 406
Day of Month: 29/7/15

AAA

Reference 4th Corps telegram G 383 yesterdays date 47th Division will also hand over to 15th Division six 95 millimetre mortars AAA addressed 47th and 15th Division

From: Fourth Corps
Time: 10.40 am

Lt A. Dallas

HRS 303

SECRET

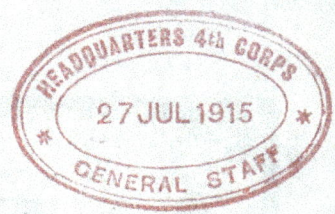

Headquarters,

    1st Army.
    1st Corps
    XXIst French Corps.

The attached copy of IVth Corps letter numbered as above regarding the relief of the 47th Division by the 15th Division, is forwarded for your information.

(Sd) A.G. Dallas BGGS
for

27th July, 1915.

Lieutenant General,
Commanding IVth Corps.

SECRET

IVth Corps No. H.R.S. 303

Copy

1st Division.
47th Division.
15th Division.

[Stamp: HEADQUARTERS 4th CORPS, 27 JUL 1915, GENERAL STAFF]

    The 15th Division will relieve the 47th Division in Sections "W" and "X" as detailed below, under arrangements to be made between Divisions.

    On relief by the 15th Division the 47th Division will move into the area now occupied by the 15th Division.

(a)   Sections W.1., W.2., and W.3., will be relieved by one Brigade on the night of the 2nd/3rd August.

(b)   Sections X.1., and X.2., will be relieved by one Brigade on the night of the 3rd/4th August.

(c)   The reserve Brigade 47th Division will be relieved by one Brigade of the 15th Division on the 3rd August.

2.   The moves of the Divisional Troops of both the 15th and 47th Divisions will be arranged between Divisions.

3.   The Headquarters and Field Companies R.E. 47th Division will take over the billets now occupied by the Headquarters and Field Companies R.E. of the 15th Division.

    The C.R.E. 47th Division will take charge of the work on the SAILLY LABOURSE line.

4.   All moves/

4.   All moves will be completed before 6 a.m. on the 4th August, when the G.O.C. 15th Division will assume responsibility for the defence of the line.

(Sd) AJGDalla

27th July, 1915.

Brigadier General,
General Staff, IVth Corps.

SECRET

IVth Corps No. H.R.S. HRS 303

Headquarters,

    47th Division.

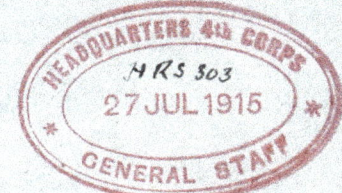

The attached copy of IVth Corps memorandum numbered as above of today's date addressed to the 15th Division is forwarded for your information with reference to paragraph 5.

(Sd) AgDallas

27th July, 1915.
                              Brigadier General,
                          General Staff, IVth Corps.

SECRET

IVth Corps No.

Copy

15th Division.

With reference to your 64/G dated 25th inst:-

Para: 1. Noted.

Para: 2. The best arrangements to meet the circumstances of the case must be made within the billeting area allotted.

Para: 3. (a) (b) and (c) noted.

(d) These must be located West of the VAUDRICCOURT - HOUCHIN spur as the MOULIN ROUGE - GOSNAY line is too far back.

(e) The BOIS DE DAMES will be outside the 15th Division new billeting area and cannot be used.

Para: 4. See new billeting area map forwarded to you today.

Para: 5. The C.R.A. 47th Division will remain responsible for the Artillery defence of the 47th Division front, under the orders of the G.O.C., 47th Division, up till 6 a.m. on the morning of the 4th August, when the G.O.C. 15th Division assumes responsibility for the defence of the line.

The C.R.A. 15th Division will be in close touch with the C.R.A. 47th Division until he becomes responsible for the Artillery defence of the line.

(Sd) A.J. Dallas

H.Q., 4th Corps.
27th July, 1915.

Brigadier General,
General Staff, 4th Corps.

SECRET

IVth Corps No.

15th Division.

With reference to your 64/G dated 25th inst:-

Para: 1. Noted.

Para: 2. The best arrangements to meet the circumstances of the case must be made within the billeting area allotted.

Para: 3. (a) (b) and (c) noted.

(d) These must be located West of the VAUDRIC-COURT — HOUCHIN spur as the MOULIN ROUGE — GOSNAY line is too far back.

(e) The BOIS DE DAMES will be outside the 15th Division new billeting area and cannot be used.

Para: 4. See new billeting area map forwarded to you today.

Para: 5. The C.R.A. 47th Division will remain responsible for the Artillery defence of the 47th Division front, under the orders of the G.O.C., 47th Division, up till 6 a.m. on the morning of the 4th August, when the G.O.C. 15th Division assumes responsibility for the defence of the line. The C.R.A. 15th Division will be in close touch with the C.R.A. 47th Division until he becomes responsible for the Artillery defence of the line.

H.Q., 4th Corps.
27th July, 1915.

Brigadier General,
General Staff, 4th Corps.

1st Division.
15th Division.
47th Division.

1. With a view to the introduction of the 15th Division into the trench line at an early date, arrangements will be made by the 1st and 47th Divisions, with the 15th Division, for the necessary instruction of the latter.

It is the intention of the Corps Commander that the 15th Division shall take over the present front now held by the 47th Division, but in order to give more varied experience in the methods of trench warfare generally, the instruction will be undertaken by both the 1st and 47th Divisions.

2. Commencing on the 20th instant, the programme for instruction will be as follows:-

(a) Brigade Commanders and their Staffs, Battalion Commanders, Seconds in Command, Adjutants and a proportion of selected N.C.O's will be attached from each Brigade of the 15th Division in turn, to similar units of the 1st Division in Sections Y.1., Y.2 and Y.3. They will then pass on to the 47th Division to acquaint themselves with the conditions of the trench line they will be required to hold.

Attachments in all cases will be for two days.

(b) The instruction of the companies of infantry of the 15th Division will be carried out with the battalions of both Brigades of the 47th Division holding the trench line; two platoons from each company selected being attached, for two days, to

/each

each of the companies of the battalions of the 47th Division. Sixteen companies should thus be trained in four days and, similarly, the 48 companies in 12 days.

(c) Artillery. Each battery of the 15th Division will send a complete section to replace a section of a corresponding battery of the 1st Division. This section will remain in action for a period of four days, when it will be withdrawn prior to the relief of the artillery of the 47th Division.

While the section of batteries of the 15th Division are in action on the 1st Division front, the sections of the latter will be temporarily withdrawn out of action.

Artillery officers whose sections are not in action with the 1st Division and who are available, will make themselves acquainted with the 47th Division front and gun positions with a view to taking over the defence of the line later on.

3. With regard to the instruction generally, every care should be taken to ensure that the officers and Non-commissioned officers are enabled to gain a thorough knowledge of their respective duties.

Officers and Non-commissioned Officers must, if possible, be placed for instruction with individuals responsible for performing the duties they themselves will have to perform on taking over; Battalion Commanders should be attached to Battalion Commanders, Company Commanders to Company Commanders, and so on.

/4.

4. Officers and Non-commissioned Officers, during their attachment, will be instructed generally in all the principles of trench warfare, such as the construction and maintenance of trenches, siting of loopholes, employment of machine-guns and snipers, erection of obstacles, drainage and sanitation. They will further be instructed particularly in the exact topography of the portion of the trenches their units will occupy. The details of the siting of the enemy's trenches opposite, so far as they are known, should be pointed out to them, especially places from which sniper's or machine-gun fire may be expected, places from which saps have been, or seem likely to be, commenced, etc.

5. The method of carrying out reliefs, and the routes followed, must be carefully explained to officers and non-commissioned officers, and it must be ensured by actual experiment that they can find their way in and out of the trenches in the dark.

They must also be shown the best methods of bringing up rations, water, ammunition, R.E.stores, and all other trench requirements.

6. Six motor busses are at the disposal of the IVth Corps and can be obtained on demand for the purpose of transporting parties from the more distant billets to any suitable point.

(Sd) A.G. Dallas.

H.Q., IVth Corps.
19th July, 1915.

Brigadier-General,
General Staff, 4th Corps.

DRAFT.

3 Divisions.

1. With a view to the introduction of the 15th Division into the trench line at an early date, arrangements will be made by the 1st and 47th Divisions, with the 15th Division, for the necessary instruction of the latter.

It is the intention of the Corps Commander that the 15th Division shall take over the present ~~trench line~~ front now held by the 47th Division, but in order to give more varied experience, ~~the necessary instruction in~~ in the methods of trench warfare generally the instructions will be undertaken by both the 1st and 47th Divisions.

2. Commencing on the 20th instant, the programme for instruction will be as follows:-

(a) Brigade Commanders and their Staffs, Battalion Commanders, Seconds in Command, Adjutants and a proportion of selected N.C.O's will be attached from each Brigade of the 15th Division in turn, to similar units of the 1st Division in Sections Y.1., Y.2 and Y.3. They will then pass on to the 47th Division to acquaint themselves with the ~~exact~~ conditions of the trench line they will be required ~~are~~ to hold.

Attachments in all ~~both~~ cases will be for three ~~two~~ days.

(b) The instruction of the companies of infantry of the 15th Division will be carried out with the Battalions of both Brigades of the 47th Division holding the trench line; two platoons from each company selected being attached, for ~~two~~ days, to each of the companies of the ~~~~ battalions of the 47th Division. Sixteen ~~Twenty~~ companies should thus be trained in four days and, similarly, the 48 companies in 12 days.

(c) <u>Artillery</u>. Each battery of the 15th Division will send a complete section to replace a section

/of

of a corresponding battery of the 1st Division. This section will remain in action for a period of four days, when it will be withdrawn prior to the relief of the Artillery of the 47th Division.

While the section of batteries of the 15th Division are in action on the 1st Division front, the sections of the latter will be temporarily withdrawn out of action.

Artillery officers whose sections are not in action with the 1st Division and who are available will make themselves acquainted with the 47th Division front and gun positions with a view to taking over the defence of the line later on.

3. With regard to the instruction generally, every care should be taken to ensure that the Officers and Non-commissioned Officers are enabled to gain thorough knowledge of their respective duties.

Officers and Non-commissioned Officers must, if possible, be placed for instruction with individuals responsible for performing the duties they themselves will have to perform on taking over; battalion commanders should be attached to battalion commanders, company commanders to company commanders, and so on.

4. Officers and Non-commissioned Officers, during their attachment, will be instructed generally in all the principles of trench warfare such as the construction and maintenance of trenches, siting of loopholes, employment of machine guns and snipers, erection of obstacles, drainage, and sanitation. They will further be instructed particularly in the exact topography of the portion of the trenches their units will occupy. The details of the siting of the enemy's trenches opposite, so far as they are known, should be pointed out to

them/

them, especially places from which sniper's or machine gun fire may be expected, places from which saps have been, or seem likely to be, commenced, etc.

5. The method of carrying out reliefs, and the routes followed, must be carefully explained to Officers and Non-commissioned Officers, and it must be ensured by actual experiment that they can find their way in and out of the trenches in the dark.

They must also be shown the best methods of bringing up rations, water, ammunition, R.E. stores, and all other trench requirements.

6. Six motor buses are at the disposal of the IVth Corps and can be obtained on demand for the purpose of transporting parties from their more distant billets to any suitable point.

ARTILLERY - 15th DIVISION

Showing dates of introduction to 1st Division line for instruction

---

<u>JULY</u>

70th Brigade 18 pr.	"A" 70th Battery	1 Section 20/21st to 51st Battery.
	"B" -:-	
	"C" -:-	1 Section 20/21st to 116th Battery.
	"D" -:-	1 Section 20/21st to 117th Battery.
71st Brigade 18 pr.	"A" 71st Battery	1 Section 20/21st to 113th Battery.
	"B" -:-	1 Section 20/21st to 114th Battery.
	"C" -:-	
	"D" -:-	
72nd Brigade	"A" 72nd Battery	1 Section 20/21st to 46th Battery.
	"B" -:-	1 Section 20/21st to 115th Battery.
	"C" -:-	
	"D" -:-	
73rd Brigade 4.5" How.	"A" 73rd Battery	1 Section 20/21st to 40th Battery.
	"B" -:-	1 Section 20/21st to 30th Battery.
	"C" -:-	
	"D" -:-	

SECRET

4th Corps H.R.S. 303.

HRS 303

15th Division.

A copy of correspondence received from the 47th Division together with 4th Corps reply thereto is forwarded herewith for your information and compliance.

(sd) A.J. Dallas

Brigadier General,
General Staff, 4th Corps.

24th July, 1915.

SECRET

HRS 303

4th Corps H.R.S. 303.

Copy

47th Division.

With reference to your G/317/4 dated the 23rd inst. forwarding a minute by the C.R.A. 47th Division regarding the relief of the batteries of the 47th Division by those of the 15th Division, the Corps Commander has decided that complete Sections should go directly from the battery positions with the 1st Division to those of the 47th Division after their period of instruction has been completed.

With regard to the question of the handing over of telephone wires, see 4th Corps No.855 (G) dated 23/7/15 which has been already forwarded to you.

(sd) Aly Dallas

Brigadier General,
General Staff, 4th Corps.

24th July, 1915.

HRS 303

SECRET

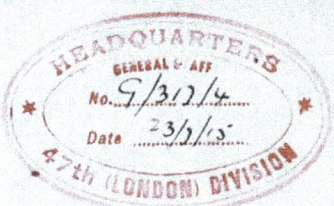

To Headquarters,
    47th. (London) Division.

Re relief of batteries of 47th. Division by those of the 15th. Division.

1. I have discussed this matter with the G.O.C.R.A., 15th. Division.

2. It is proposed that as regards new positions that he can send in whole batteries as soon as these positions are completed.

3. As regards the positions now occupied by the 47th. Divl. Artillery, I suggest that in each battery, 1 gun of the 15th. Division should come in the first night and the other 3 guns the following night. This leaves the front protected by not less than 3 guns already registered.

4. Working parties of the 15th. Division Artillery will have to be sent up to prepare new positions. I am already preparing 5 new Battery positions besides strengthening the old French positions, so have no more labour available.

5. I understand that the 15th. Divisional Artillery have very little telephone wire.
   If we leave our wires down, it must be on the understanding that a similar amount of new wire is supplied, otherwise I shall be compelled to recover my existing lines, some of which have been buried.

Cuil Dray
Brigadier-General,
Comdg. 47th. Divl. Artillery.

B.M. c/853
22/7/15.

4th Corps.
Forwarded with reference to your No 832 G para 2(c) of 19th inst.
23.7.15
W. Ruthven Lt Col GS
47th Divn

Copy

HRS303

4th Corps No.832 (G).

1st Division.
15th Division.
47th Division.
----

1. With reference to 4th Corps No.832 (G) dated 19/7/15, as soon as the Sections of Batteries have completed their 4 days of instruction with the 1st Division they will move into action in the 47th Division area under arrangements to be made between Divisions. These Sections will remain in action and will undertake the necessary registration on the 47th Division front in anticipation of the replacement of the Artillery of the 47th Division by that of the 15th Division. The registration will be carried out by degrees so as to avoid any abnormal increase of artillery fire.

2. Divisions will report to 4th Corps Headquarters, as soon as they take place, all movements of Artillery Sections into position in the 1st Division area and subsequently from the 1st Division area to that of the 47th Division.

(Sd) AJ Dallas

Brigadier General,
General Staff, 4th Corps.

20th July, 1915.

4th Corps No.832 (G).

1st Division.
15th Division.
47th Division.
----

1. With reference to 4th Corps No.832 (G) dated 19/7/15, as soon as the Sections of Batteries have completed their 4 days of instruction with the 1st Division they will move into action in the 47th Division area under arrangements to be made between Divisions. These Sections will remain in action and will undertake the necessary registration on the 47th Division front in anticipation of the replacement of the Artillery of the 47th Division by that of the 15th Division. The registration will be carried out by degrees so as to avoid any abnormal increase of artillery fire.

2. Divisions will report to 4th Corps Headquarters, as soon as they take place, all movements of Artillery Sections into position in the 1st Division area and subsequently from the 1st Division area to that of the 47th Division.

20th July, 1915.

Brigadier General,
General Staff, 4th Corps.

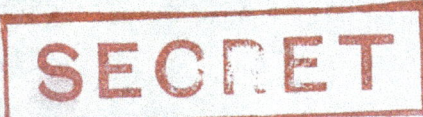

HRS 303

1st Divn. No. 394 (G).

4th Corps.

With reference to para. 2 of your No. 832 (G), dated 20th July, 1915, seven Sections of 18 pr. guns and two Sections of 4.5" Howitzers of the 15th Division moved into action in the 1st Division area at 10 p.m. 20th July.

21/7/15.

W.G. Woodbine Capt
f/ Major General,
Commanding 1st Division.

15th Division 19/G

Fourth Corps.

Forwarded for information - your 832/G dated 19/7/15.

E. G. Henderson,

H.Q. 15th Division.
20th July 1915.

Major,
General Staff, 15th Division.

15th Division 19/G.

44th)
45th) Inf.Bdes.
46th)

With reference to attached instructions from 4th Corps, the attachment of platoons to companies of battalions of the 47th Division, will be carried out as follows:-

1. Platoons of the 44th Bde and of half the 46th Bde will be attached to the 140th Bde up to the night of 22/23rd, and after that date to the 142 Bde, which relieves the 140th.

Platoons of the 45th Bde and of the other half of the 46th Bde will be attached to the 141st Bde.

Details of the tours in the trenches are given in Table "A" (attached).

Each company will send its four platoons under the platoon commanders; the company commander will accompany two of his platoons and send his captain with the other two.

Officers and men will take nothing with them except what they carry; men will take 120 rounds of ammunition.

Cookers will accompany companies, the horses (including those of the 46th Bde) returning before dawn to either HOUCHIN or HESDIGNEUL till required to fetch the cookers back. No other transport will be taken.

The NOEUX-LES-MINES - MAZINGARBE road will be kept clear of other traffic at the NOEUX-LES-MINES end from 8-30 to 9 p.m. and MAZINGARBE end from 9 to 9-30 p.m; each night by the 47th Division for the movement of platoons to and from the trenches.

46th Bde
Companies coming from the ~~trenches~~ will march as far as HOUCHIN by daylight, rest there, and go forward at dusk.

Guides will meet platoons at MAZINGARBE, or as arranged between the Brigades concerned.

2. The arrangements for the attachment of Brigadiers and staffs (4th Corps instructions, para 2a) will be:-

6 p.m.   6 p.m.
July 20 to July 22 G.O.C. & Staff 44th Bde to 2nd Bde 1st Div.
6 p.m.   6 p.m.
July 22 to July 24.
                                    to 140th & 142nd Bde,
                                    47th Div.

2.

```
6 p.m.          6 p.m.
July 24th to    July 26    G.O.C.& Staff 46th Bde to 2nd Bde,1st Div.
6 p.m.          6 p.m.
July 26th to    July 28           do        to 141st Bde,47th Div
6 p.m.          6 p.m.
July 28th to    July 30    G.O.C.& Staff 45th Bde to 2nd Bde,1st Div.
6 p.m.          6 p.m.
July 30th to    Augt 1st          do        to 141st Bde,47th Div.
```

While attached to the 2nd Bde the G.O.C. and B.M. will be accommodated at Brigade Headquarters at NOYELLES and the remainder of the staff at the CHATEAU-DES-PRES — Officers staying at the latter place must make their own feeding arrangements.

3. The arrangements for the attachment of C.O's, 2nds in command, adjutants, machine gun officers, and selected N.C.O's are shewn in the Table "B" (attached).

10 N.C.O's will be selected from each battalion; it is suggested that these should be the 4 Coy S.M's, 4 Coy Q.M.S's and 2 M.G. N.C.O's.

4. Officers and other ranks will proceed to and from the rendezvous as shewn in the attached Table "C".

5. All individuals and platoons during their attachment, will be rationed by the Division to which they are attached.

(Sgd) J.T.BURNETT-STUART.

H.Q.15th Division.   Lieut Colonel,
20th July 1915.   General Staff.

<u>4 enclosures.</u>

4th Corps letter of 19/7/15.
Tables A, B,& C.

Table "A"
15th. Division 19/G of 20/7/1915.

Companies will go into the trenches for instruction as follows:-

RIGHT section of line

44th. Inf. Bde.
- (On the evening of the 20th.- 2 Coys 10th Gordons
-                                2 Coys 8th. Seaforths:
- "   "   "   "   "   22nd - 2 Coys 10th. Gordons
-                             2 Coys 8th. Seaforths.

46th. Inf. Bde.
- "   "   "   "   "   24th - 2 Coys 10th Sco. Rif.
-                             2 Coys 12th. H.L.I
- "   "   "   "   "   26th.- 2 Coys 10th. Sco. Rif
-                             2 Coys 12th. H.L.I.

44th. Inf. Bde.
- "   "   "   "   "   28th.- 2 Coys 7th. Camerons
-                             2 Coys 9th. Royal Highrs.
- "   "   "   "   "   30th.- 2 Coys 7th. Camerons.
-                             2 Coys 9th Royal Highrs.

LEFT section of line

45th. Inf. Bde.
- (On the evening of the 20th.- 2 Coys 11th A & S Highrs.
-                                2 Coys 6th. Camerons.
- "   "   "   "   "   22nd.- 2 Coys 11th A & S Highrs.
-                             2 Coys 6th. Camerons.

46th. Inf. Bde.
- "   "   "   "   "   24th.- 2 Coys 7th. K.O.S.B's.
-                             2 Coys 8th. K.O.S.B's.
- "   "   "   "   "   26th.- 2 Coys 7th. K.O.S.B's.
-                             2 Coys 8th. K.O.S.B's.

45th. Inf. Bde
- "   "   "   "   "   28th - 2 Coys 13th. Royal Scots.
-                             2 Coys 7th. Royal Sco. Fus.
- "   "   "   "   "   30th.- 2 Coys 13th. Royal Scots.
-                             2 Coys 7th. Royal Sco. Fus.

The 7th. Camerons (44th. Inf. Bde.) at LES BREBIS will be relieved on the night of the 24/25 by the 10th. Gordons.

The 13th. Royal Scots (45th. Inf. Bde) at MAROC will be relieved on the night of the 25/26 by the 6th. Camerons.

Table "B"

15th Division 19/G of 20/7/15.

(a) Attachment of C.O's, Adjutants and 5 Warrant Officers or N.C.O's per Battn.

Dates.	To 2nd Bde. 1st Divn.	47th Division.	Inf. Bde.
20th July – 22 Jul	8th Seaforth Highrs. 10th Gordon Highrs.	6th Cameron Highrs) 11th A & S Highrs)	141st Bde.
22nd Jul – 24 Jul	6th Cameron Highrs. 11th A & S Highrs.	8th Seaforth Highrs.) 10th Gordon Highrs.)	140th Bde.
24 July – 26th Jul	10th Scottish Rifles 12th H.L.I.	7th K.O.S.B's.) 8th K.O.S.B's.)	141st Bde.
26 July – 28 July	7th K.O.S.B's 8th K.O.S.B's	10th Scottish Rifs) 12th H.L.I.)	142nd Bde.
28 July – 30 July	7th Camerons 9th Royal Highrs	13th Royal Scots 7th Royal Sco. Fus.)	141st Bde.
30 July – Augt. 1.	13th Royal Scots. 7th Royal Sco. Fus.	7th Cameron Highrs.) 9th Royal Highrs.)	142nd Bde.

(b) Attachment of 2nds in command, M.G. Officers and 5 Warrant Officers or N.C.O's per Battalion.

Dates.	To 2nd Bde 1st Divn.	To 47th Division.	Inf. Bde.
20th Jul – 22 July	7th K.O.S.B's. 8th K.O.S.B's.	10th Scottish Rifs) 12th H.L.I.)	140th Bde.
22 July – 24 July	12th H.L.I. 10th Scottish Rifles.	7th K.O.S.B's) 8th K.O.S.B's)	141st Bde.
24 July – 26 July	13th Royal Scots. 7th Cameron Highrs.	9th Royal Highrs. 7th Royal Sco. Fus.	142nd Bde. 141st Bde.
26 July – 28 July	9th Royal Highrs. 7th Royal Sco. Fus.	13th Royal Scots) 7th Cameron Highrs.)	141st Bde. 142nd Bde
28 July – 30th Jul.	11th A & S Highrs. 10th Gordon Highrs.	8th Seaforth Highrs. 6th Cameron Highrs.	142nd Bde. 141st Bde.
30th Jul – 1 Augt.	8th Seaforth Highrs. 6th Cameron Highrs.	11th A & S Highrs. 10th Gordon Highrs.	141st Bde. 142nd Bde.

NOTE:- Each attachment is for two days beginning at 6 p.m. in the cases of attachments (a) to the 1st Division at CHATEAU-DES-PRES, SAILLY-LA-BOURSE at 6 p.m., and (b) to the 47th Division at H.Q. 140th Inf. Bde. MAZINGARBE at 7 p.m.

Table "C".

Bus, etc, arrangements.

Two buses will call on July 20th. 22nd. 24th. 26th. 28th. and 30th. at 4.15.p.m. at the road fork centre of ALLOUAGNE village at 4.15 p.m.

Attachments 1st. Division.

One bus will convey Officers and N.C.O's. to the RENDEZVOUS of the 1st. Division - CHATEAU des PRES, SAILLY LA BOURSE arriving not later than 6.p.m.

From this point the parties will be conducted by guides to their destination.

The Bus proceeding to the CHATEAU des PRES should not actually enter the grounds but halt on the main road just outside the drive. No bus should go beyond SAILLY LA BOURSE.

Attachments 47th. Division.

The other bus will proceed to the main cross roads in NOEUX les MINES arriving not later than 6.p.m. From this point officers may ride or walk to the RENDEZVOUS (H.Q.140th.Bde) in MAZINGARBE, arriving there not later than 7.p.m.

Officers of the 44th. and 45th. Inf. Bdes. will ride or walk to the RENDEZVOUS: N.C.O's will walk, arriving there not later than 7.p.m.

Grooms should be in waiting at the RENDEZVOUS, MAZINGARBE and take the horses of officers back to their units. No bus will proceed beyond NOEUX les MINES.

Attachments Both Divisions.

On July 22nd. 24th. 26th. 28th. and 30th. the buses will wait at the RENDEZVOUS and will be available to convey officers to the other Division or in the case of officers of the 46th. Bde. who have completed both attachments, back to their units. Officers of the 44th. and 45th. Inf. Bdes. will make their own arrangements to return to their units on completion of their attachments.

Officers and N.C.O's will transfer from one Division to another under their own arrangements.

On August 1st. one bus will proceed direct to each RENDEZVOUS reporting at 7.p.m. and pick up officers of the 46th. Inf. Bde.

15th Division 19/G.

44th)
45th) Inf.Bdes.
46th)

With reference to attached instructions from 4th Corps, the attachment of platoons to companies of battalions of the 47th Division, will be carried out as follows:-

1. Platoons of the 44th Bde and of half the 46th Bde will be attached to the 140th Bde up to the night of 22/23 rd, and after that date to the 142 Bde, which relieves the 140th.

Platoons of the 45th Bde and of the other half of the 46th Bde will be attached to the 141st Bde.

Details of the tours in the trenches are given in Table "A" (attached).

Each company will send its four platoons under the platoon commanders; the company commander will accompany two of his platoons and send his captain with the other two.

Officers and men will take nothing with them except what they carry; men will take 120 rounds of ammunition.

Cookers will accompany companies, the horses (including those of the 46th Bde) returning before dawn to either HOUCHIN or HESDIGNEUL till required to fetch the cookers back. No other transport will be taken.

The NOEUX-LES-MINES - MAZINGARBE road will be kept clear of other traffic at the NOEUX-LES-MINES end from 8-30 to 9 p.m. and MAZINGARBE end from 9 to 9-30 p.m. each night by the 47th Division for the movement of platoons to and from the trenches.

46th Bde
Companies coming from the ~~trenches~~ will march as far as HOUCHIN by daylight, rest there, and go forward at dusk.

Guides will meet platoons at MAZINGARBE, or as arranged between the Brigades concerned.

2. The arrangements for the attachment of Brigadiers and staffs (4th Corps instructions, para 2a) will be:-

6 p.m.   6 p.m.
July 20 to July 22 G.O.C. & Staff 44th Bde to 2nd Bde ~~4th~~ Div.
6 p.m.   6 p.m.
July 22 to July 24.   do   to 140th & 142nd Bde,
                                                47th Div.

2.

6 p.m.	6 p.m.		
July 24th	to July 26	G.O.C.&.Staff 46th Bde	to 2nd Bde, 1st Div.
6 p.m.	6 p.m.		
July 26th	to July 28	do	to 141st Bde, 47th Div
6 p.m.	6 p.m.		
July 28th	to July 30	G.O.C.&.Staff 45th Bde	to 2nd Bde, 1st Div.
6 p.m.	6 p.m.		
July 30th	to Augt 1st	do	to 141st Bde, 47th Div.

While attached to the 2nd Bde the G.O.C. and B.M. will be accommodated at Brigade Headquarters at NOYELLES and the remainder of the staff at the CHATEAU-DES-PRES — Officers staying at the latter place must make their own feeding arrangements.

3. The arrangements for the attachment of C.O's, 2nds in command, adjutants, machine gun officers, and selected N.C.O's are shewn in the Table "B" (attached).

10 N.C.O's will be selected from each battalion; it is suggested that these should be the 4 Coy S.M's, 4 Coy Q.M.S's and 2 M.G. N.C.O's.

4. Officers and other ranks will ~~be conveyed~~ proceed to and from the rendezvous as shewn in the attached ~~time table of busses~~ Table "C".

5. All individuals and platoons during their attachment, will be rationed by the Division to which they are attached.

                                          (Sgd) J.T.BURNETT-STUART.

H.Q.15th Division.   Lieut Colonel,

20th July 1915.   General Staff.

4 enclosures.

4th Corps letter of 19/7/15.
Tables A, B, & C.

Table "A"

15th. Division 19/G of 20/7/1915.

Companies will go into the trenches for instruction as follows:-

RIGHT section of line

44th. Inf. Bde.
(On the evening of the 20th.- 2 Coys 10th Gordons
                              2 Coys 8th. Seaforths.
"   "   "   "   " 22nd - 2 Coys 10th. Gordons
                        2 Coys 8th. Seaforths.

46th. Inf. Bde.
"   "   "   "   " 24th - 2 Coys 10th Sco. Rif.
                        2 Coys 12th. H.L.I
"   "   "   "   " 26th.- 2 Coys 10th. Sco. Rif
                         2 Coys 12th. H.L.I.

44th. Inf. Bde.
"   "   "   "   " 28th.- 2 Coys 7th. Camerons
                         2 Coys 9th. Royal Highrs.
"   "   "   "   " 30th.- 2 Coys 7th. Camerons.
                         2 Coys 9th Royal Highrs.

LEFT section of line.

45th. Inf. Bde.
(On the evening of the 20th.- 2 Coys 11th A & S Highrs.
                              2 Coys 6th. Camerons.
"   "   "   "   " 22nd.- 2 Coys 11th A & S Highrs.
                         2 Coys 6th. Camerons.

46th. Inf. Bde.
"   "   "   "   " 24th.- 2 Coys 7th. K.O.S.B's.
                         2 Coys 8th. K.O.S.B's.
"   "   "   "   " 26th.- 2 Coys 7th. K.O.S.B's.
                         2 Coys 8th. K.O.S.B's.

45th. Inf. Bde
"   "   "   "   " 28th - 2 Coys 13th. Royal Scots.
                         2 Coys 7th. Royal Sco. Fus.
"   "   "   "   " 30th.- 2 Coys 13th. Royal Scots.
                         2 Coys 7th. Royal Sco. Fus.

The 7th. Camerons (44th. Inf. Bde.) at LES BREBIS will be relieved on the night of the 24/25 by the 10th. Gordons.

The 13th. Royal Scots (45th. Inf. Bde) at MAROC will be relieved on the night of the 25/26 by the 6th. Camerons.

Table "B"

15th Division 19/G of 20/7/15.

(a) Attachment of C.O's, Adjutants and 5 Warrant Officers or N.C.O's per Battn.

Dates.	To 2nd Bde.1st Divn.	47th Division.	Inf.Bde.
20th July – 22 Jul	8th Seaforth Highrs. 10th Gordon Highrs.	6th Cameron Highrs) 11th A & S Highrs)	141st Bde.
22nd Jul – 24 Jul	6th Cameron Highrs. 11th A & S Highrs.	8th Seaforth Highrs.) 10th Gordon Highrs.)	140th Bde.
24 July – 26th Jul	10th Scottish Rifles 12th H.L.I.	7th K.O.S.B's.) 8th K.O.S.B's.)	141st Bde.
26 July – 28 July	7th K.O.S.B's 8th K.O.S.B's	10th Scottish Rifs) 12th H.L.I.)	142nd Bde.
28 July – 30 July	7th Camerons 9th Royaln Highrs	13th Royal Scots) 7th Royal Sco.Fus.)	141st Bde.
30 July – Aug 1.	13th Royal Scots. 7th Royal Sco. Fus.	7th Cameron Highrs.) 9th Royal Highrs.)	142nd Bde.

(b) Attachment of 2nds in command, M.G.Officers and 5 Warrant Officers or N.C.O's per Battalion.

Dates.	To 2nd Bde 1st Divn.	To 47th Division.	Inf. Bde.
20th Jul – 22 July	7th K.O.S.B's. 8th K.O.S.B's.	10th Scottish Rifs.) 12th H.L.I.)	140th Bde.
22 July – 24 July	12th H.L.I. 10th Scottish Rifles.	7th K.O.S.B's) 8th K.O.S.B's)	141st Bde.
24 July – 26 July	13th Royal Scots. 7th Cameron Highrs.	9th Royal Highrs. 7th Royal Sco. Fus.	142nd Bde. 141st Bde.
26 July – 28 July	9th Royal Highrs. 7th Royal Sco. Fus.	13th Royal Scots 7th Cameron Highrs.)	141st Bde. 142nd Bde.
28 July – 30th Jul.	11th A & S Highrs. 10th Gordon Highrs.	8th Seaforth Highrs. 6th Cameron Highrs.	142nd Bde. 141st Bde.
30th Jul – 1 Aug.	8th Seaforth Highrs. 6th Cameron Highrs.	11th A & S Highrs. 10th Gordon Highrs.	141st Bde. 142nd Bde.

NOTE:— Each attachment is for two days beginning at 6 p.m. in the cases of attachments (a) to the 1st Division at CHATEAU-DES-PRES, SAILLY-LA-BOURSE at 6 p.m., and (b) to the 47th Division at H.Q. 140th Inf. Bde. MAZINGARBE at 7 p.m.

Table "C".

Bus, etc, arrangements.

Two buses will call on July 20th. 22nd. 24th. 26th. 28th. and 30th. at 4.15.p.m. at the road fork centre of ALLOUAGNE ~~village at 4.15.p.m~~

Attachments 1st. Division.

One bus will convey Officers and N.C.O"s. to the RENDEZVOUS of the 1st. Division - CHATEAU des PRES, SAILLY LA BOURSE arriving not later than 6.p.m.

From this point the parties will be conducted by guides to their destination.

The Bus proceeding to the CHATEAU des PRES should not actually enter the grounds but halt on the main road just outside the drive. No bus should go beyond SAILLY LA BOURSE.

Attachments 47th. Division.

The other bus will proceed to the main cross roads in NOEUX les MINES arriving not later than 6.p.m. From this point officers may ride or walk to the RENDEZVOUS (H.Q.140th.Bde) in MAZINGARBE, arriving there not later than 7.p.m.

Officers of the 44th. and 45th. Inf. Bdes. will ride or walk to the RENDEZVOUS: N.C.O's will walk, arriving there not later than 7.p.m.

Grooms should be in waiting at the RENDEZVOUS, MAZINGARBE and take the horses of officers back to their units. No bus will proceed beyond NOEUX les MINES.

Attachments Both Divisions.

On July 22nd. 24th. 26th. 28th. and 30th. the buses will wait at the RENDEZVOUS and will be available to convey officers to the other Division or in the case of officers of the 46th. Bde. who have completed both attachments, back to their units. Officers of the 44th. and 45th. Inf. Bdes. will make their own arrangements to return to their units on completion of their attachments.

Officers and N.C.O's will transfer from one Division to another under their own arrangements.

On August 1st. one bus will proceed direct to each RENDEZVOUS reporting at 7.p.m. and pick up officers of the 46th. Inf. Bde.

1st Army Headquarters.

17th July, 1915.

Dear General,

With regard to the new divisions now coming out direct from Home I want to point out that these divisions although very good in some respects are very green indeed in others and require careful nursing and tuition at first. No doubt you are quite aware of this but C.G.S. has asked me to point out that it will pay well to give them good attention.

Yours sincerely,

R. Butler

Lieut. General Sir Henry Rawlinson,

RECORD OF THE 15th. (SCOTTISH) DIVISION.

Date
1914.

18th Sept.   Formed at ALDERSHOT under Major General A. WALLACE,
             C.B., Artillery and 46th Inf. Bde. at Bordon.
             Inspection of the Division by their Majestys THE
             KING AND QUEEN, accompanied by Lord Kitchener.

16th Nov.   44th Bde. moved to LIPHOOK.

Nov.   Divisional Hd. Qrs. moved to BORDON.

Dec.   Major General C.J. MACKENZIE, C.B., appointed to command
             the Division, vice Major General WALLACE, C.B., who
             proceeded to Egypt.

1915.

Jan.   9th Gordon Highrs. made Pioneer Bn., 7th Cameron
             Highrs. joined 44th Bde. in their place.

22nd Jan.   Inspection at FRENSHAM POND by M. MILLERAND and LORD
             KITCHENER.

20th Feb.   Division moved to SALISBURY PLAIN, Division Hd. Qrs.
             at CHOLDERTON. Artillery at BULFORD CAMP. 44th Bde.
             Hd. Qrs. and 2 Bns at DRAYCOTT CAMP, 2 Bns at
             CIRENCESTER. 45th Bde. BASINGSTOKE. Hd. Qrs. 46th
             Bde. and 3 Bns. at WINCHESTER, 12th H.L.I. ROMSEY.

22nd March. Major General F.W.N. McCRACKEN appointed to command the
             Division vice Major General MACKENZIE, to War Office.

21st April. Divisional Hd. Qrs. moved to MARLBOROUGH. 44th and 45th
             Bdes. to huts at CHISLEDON CAMP, near SWINDON. 46th
             Bde. to PARKHOUSE CAMP, near BULFORD.

21st June.   Division inspected by H.M. KING GEORGE between PERHAM
             DOWN AND TIDWORTH.

8th July.   Embarked for FRANCE.
             Billeted in the neighbourhood of ST. OMER.
             Marched and joined IVth. Corps (Lt. General Sir H.
             RAWLINSON) with Divisional Hd. Qrs. at GOSNAY.

Aug.	Took over section of the trenches opposite LOOS from 47th (London) Division, with French troops on the Right and 1st Division on the Left. Divl. Hd. Qrs. DOUVRIN.
Sept.	47th Division took over the next sector on the Right between the 15th Division and the French.
24th Sept.	Advanced Divl. Hd. Qrs. at MAZINGARBE.
25th Sept.	15th Division attacked and took the village of LOOS and HILL 70. Casualties about 6,000.
27th Sept.	Division relieved and billeted in neighbourhood of LILLERS. Divl. Hd. Qrs. at LABUISSIERE.
21st Octo.	Having received large reinforcements, the Division relieved the 12th Division in the line opposite the HOHENZOLLERN REDOUBT.
15th Dec.	Division relieved by the 47th (LONDON) Division and proceeded to billets in LILLERS AREA for a rest. Divl. Hd. Qrs. at CHATEAU PHILOMEL, LILLERS.
1916	
15th Jan.	Division took over the centre sector in the LOOS Salient, relieving the 1st Division. with Hd. Qrs. at MAZINGARBE.
Feb.	Lt. General Sir . . WILSON appointed to command IVth Corps, vice Sir H. RAWLINSON to command Fourth Army.
2nd March.	Division posted to 1st Corps (Lt. General Sir H. GOUGH).
25th March.	Division relieved in LOOS Salient by 16th Division and moved by train to LILLERS AREA, Div. Hd. Qrs. at CHATEAU PHILOMEL. Lt. General KAVANAGH appointed to command. First Corps vice Lt. General Si. H. Gough. Part of Division inspected by General JOFFRE near ESTREE BLANCHE.
27th April.	Division relieved 12th Division in the HOHENZOLLERN Sector. Divl. Hd. Qrs. at SAILLY LABOURSE.

11th May.	German attack on "THE KINK."
	10/11th H.L.I. joined the Div. from 9th Div.
22nd July and 23rd July.	Division relieved by 8th Division on the Right, and 16th Division on the Left, and marched to billets at HEUCHIN, TANGRY, MARLES LES MINES, LAPOUGNOY. Division Hd. Qrs. at CHATEAU BRYAS.
24th July.	Division marched via FREVENT - BERNAVILLE - VIGNACOURT ST. GRATIEN - BRAIZIEUX, joining IIIrd Corps (Lt.Gen. PULTENEY) of Fourth Army. (Sir H. RAWLINSON).
8th Aug.	Division took over the front line opposite MARTINPUICH relieving the 23rd Division.
12th - 17th Aug.	Operations resulting in capture of the SWITCH LINE.
30th Aug.	Capture of INTERMEDIATE LINE and 4 Officers and 123 O.Rs.
15th Sept.	The Division captured MARTINPUICH, and three lines of trenches, taking 600-700 prisoners, 13 machine guns, three heavy Howitzers, three 77 mm. guns, and one Trench mortar, also a quantity of R. E. Material. Casualties about 1800.
19th Sept.	Division relieved by 23rd Division and went to billets with Hd. Qrs. at MONTIGNY.
9th Oct.	Division relieved the 23rd Division in the front line (LE SARS).
3rd Nov.	Division relieved by 48th Division and proceeded to billets. HD. Qrs. at BAIZIEUX CHATEAU.
1st Dece.	Division relieved 50th Division in IIIrd Corps Reserve area. Hd. Qrs. ALBERT.
16th Dec.	Division relieved 48th Division in the front line, LE SARS Sector IIIrd Corps front.
1917	
3rd Feb.	Relieved by 2nd Australian Division and proceeded to billets in Fricourt area. Divl. Hd. Qrs. at BAIZIEUX.

4.

18th Feb.	Concentrated DUISANS area, Artillery in St. MICHEL. Hd. Qrs. at DUISANS. Division now in VIth. Corps (Lt. General J.A.H. HALDANE), and Third Army, (General Sir E.H.H. ALLENBY.)
24th Feb.	Took over front line of VIth. Corps Sector (East of ARRAS) from 12th Division.
9th April to 11th April.	Took part in attack on MONCHY LE PREUX, on the 11th. The C. in C. visited the Division and congratulated it in its performances.
12th April.	Relieved by the 17th Division and billeted in ARRAS and DUISANS.
18th April.	Division Hd. Qrs. moved to WAGONLIEU.
23rd April.	Took part in attack E. of ARRAS and capture of BLUE LINE.
29th April.	Relieved in line by 56th Division and proceeded to ARRAS, thence to DUISANS, SIMONCOURT, and BERNEVILLE. Div. Hd. Qrs. at WARLUS in VIth Corps Reserve.
6th May.	Transferred to XVIIIth Corps (Lt. General) Divl. Artillery remained in the line under 56th Div.
8th May.	Hd. Qrs. at LE CAUROY, units of Division at GRAND HILLECOURT - SUS St. LAGER - BARLY - WANQUETIN - GOUY EN ARTOIS.
17th May.	Transferred to XIXth Corps. (Lt. General) Fifth Army.
21st May.	Hd. Qrs. at WILLEMAN units at REBOEUVRE - BOUQUE MAISON - BONNIERES - SUS ST. LEGER - FONTAINE L'ETALON - NOEUX and OEUF.
17th June.	Major General F.W.N. McCracken, K.C.B. D.S.O., left the Division (after commanding it for over two years) to command XIIIth Corps. Succeeded by Major General H.F. THUILLIER, C.B., C.M.G.

29th June.	Relieved 55th Division in the Right Sector of XIXth Corps front (YPRES-ROULERS Road) H.Q. at VLAMERTINGHE.
31st July.	Took part in the attack on FREZENBERG. Casualties 3581.
xxxx	Insert here.
19th Aug. to 29th Aug.	Took part in the attacks by XIXth Corps in YPRES Salient Casualties 2688.
31st Aug.	Relieved by 42nd Division and proceeded to WORMHOUDT AREA. Hd. Qrs. at WATOU.
2nd Sept.	Transferred from XIXth Corps, Fifth Army, to XVIIth. Corps (Lt. General Sir C. FERGUSSON), Third Army.
8th Sept.	Relieved 4th Division in front line E. of ARRAS. Hd. Qrs. ARRAS.
10th Oct.	Major General H.F. THUILLIER relinquished command of the Division on appointment to Ministry of Munitions, succeeded by Major General H.L. REED V.C., C.M.G.
1918 3rd Jan.	Relieved by Guards Division and moved to billets in DAINVILLE - SIMENCOURT - BERNAVILLE - HABARCQ.
7th Jan. to 4th Feb.	Re-fitting and training. Hd. Qrs. at NOYELLE VION.
7th Feb.	Took over Right Sector, XVIIth. Corps front, East of ARRAS from 4th Division. Hd. Qrs. at ARRAS.
28th March.	German attack on XVIIth Corps front, casualties 2317.
29th March.	Messages received from Corps Commander, Sir C. Fergusson.
24th April.	Relieved by 56th Division and proceeded by bus and road to XIIIth Corps area, (LT. General) in First Army Reserve, Hd. Qrs. at AUCHEL.
May	Transferred from XIIIth Corps to XVIIth Corps.
6th May.	Relieved 1st Canadian Division in front line E. of ARRAS Hd. Qrs. at ETRUN.
14th July.	Relieved by 1st Canadian Division and billeted in VILLERS CHATEL area prior to joining Third French Army.

18th July.	Division transferred to Third French Army and from that to Tenth French Army.
22nd July.	Concentrated in St. PIERRE AIGLE area. Hd. Qrs. at COEUVRES.
23rd July to 3rd Aug.	Relieved 1st U.S.A. Division in the line W. of BUZANCY, (Left Sector XXth French Corps), and took part in the attack on and capture of BUZANCY and neighbouring villages. Casualties 3516.
3rd Aug.	Relieved by 17th Division and concentrated with Div. Hd. Qrs. at VIERZY.
7th Aug.	Special ORDRE GENERAL issued by General MANGIN.
8th Aug.	Division came under orders of XXIIth Corps and concentrated in area AMBRINES -, BEAUFORT - MAZIERES. Hd.Qrs. at LE CAUROY.
Aug.	Transferred from XXIIth Corps to XVIIth Corps.
18th Aug.	Relieved 56th Division in front line E. of ARRAS. HD. Qrs. at WARLUS.
23rd Aug.	Relieved by 2nd and 3rd Canadian Divisions and proceeded to join 1st Corps, First Army.
26th Aug.	Hd. Qrs. at BRAQUEMONT. Division relieved 11th Division in the front line in the LOOS SALIENT.
11th Sept. to 20th Sept.	Hard fighting round the QUARRIES which were captured by the 45th Bde. on Sept. 11th.
21st Sept.	1st Corps transferred from First Army to Fifth Army.
2nd Oct.	Division advanced to West of VENDIN - DOUVRIN line,
16th Oct.	Advance continued.
21st Oct.	Hd. Qrs. at GENECH CHATEAU. Advance held up by enemy rear guards E. of Canal.
25th Oct.	Hd. Qrs. at LA GLANERIE.
8th Nov.	Canal crossed by 44th Bde.
9th Nov.	Advance continued.
11th Nov.	Hostilities ceased at 11 A.M. and Division halted on line E. of PERUWELZ - LEUZE, with Div. Hd. Qrs. at TOURPES.